My Adolescent Thoughts

Holly Marie

India | USA | UK

Dedication

To Mrs.Gover,

You believed in me when I didn't believe in myself. You saw me for what my soul was, not who I tried to be. Everyone has a spark, and you helped me find mine when I was lost. You helped me grow from the shy, lonely girl I was freshman year to the powerful, confident senior I am now. And for that I am eternally grateful.

Preface

"My Adolescent Thoughts" by Holly Marie is a collection of poems that reflect her personal feelings toward herself and other aspects in her life, along with some of her relationships to others. As you read from poem to poem and verse to verse put yourself in her shoes, or don't. Listen to what she's trying to say, and why not answer back in the margins. Words on a page are nothing if not read. Why not go in deep? Understand what she is laying down, and why she says it. This collection can be funny, serious, or just heartbreaking knowing that someone has felt what you, yourself have felt. Now please sit back, relax, and enjoy the mind of Holly Marie.

Acknowledgements

Thank you to all of those in my life who have pushed me
to do my best and cheered me on, it is because of you,
that I will succeed.

1. My God

When I sit with tsunami eyes, and a red nose
I pray to the god who fixes a bad hair day,
I pray to the bestfriend-for-a-day god,
The oh-he-broke-your-heart-I'll-break-his-nose god.
I sit hazy-eyed with the narration of all my decisions for
the past 17 years
And talk to the it's-okay-babe-shit-happens god.
To the makeup wipes-hairstylist-marvel comic- loving
god,
To the trivia-loving-one-who's-not-a-certified-
psychologist- but-gives-me-advice-anyway god.
When the tsunami clears up, I thank the anti-tsunami
god and move on.

2. Cloudy Day

Teardrops are like raindrops.
The only difference
Is these ones don't wash away,
And raindrops don't leave stains.
Lately, I've been having more storms.
Each day there are multiple showers and the sky keeps
getting cloudier.
Everyone says there's sunshine coming
And I believe them.
But my eyes have been filled with water and my head
has been shaded by the clouds.
Will I ever see the sun again?
Will a smile ever come from my frown?

3. Size M

I'm in the middle,
I'm the medium girl.
I'm too big to be called skinny yet too small to be called
fat.
I'm 3rd out of 4 kids,
I'm not the oldest or the youngest,
I'm not the smartest nor the prettiest,
I'm in the middle.
That's where I am.
I'm not first pick but not too noticeable to be last.
I have brown hair, curves and hazel eyes,
I'm not blonde, nor a stick, and again I have hazel not
blue eyes.
Time and time again I'm stuck in size M.
I wonder and yeah I know this is who I am.
I'm not 6 foot nor am I 4,
I'm 5 foot 1 and a ½,
I hope that's enough.
I label myself cause I'm not them.
I love myself cause I'm not them.
I just hope someone will love me and it won't have
anything to do with size M.

4. Complication

Life is too confusing,
Too unassuming,
Too disturbing,
And unreal.

When I walk the halls at school
Does it matter if I'm rude or cool?

If I just nod my head and fake a smile does that fix
everything?

Or If I express how I feel
Does that make me something?

And if I dress nice and speak for how I am told
Does that make me a good student, or forever old?
But see is that me?
Am I the girl who raises hands?
Am I the one who does what she's told and understands?

But life is too complicated and hesitant.

I mean I'm the complication
And I'm the one who is sad.

Why does every person here think that I'm mad?

They don't believe that someone like me
Could be broken
 From everything that they have spoken.

Because when your the nice girl
Your the one that always gets
Tagged.

5. Fed Up

I am sick of jumping over the puddles I cried.
I am tired of holding onto the balloon that is my heart,
 that is too small for me, yet too big for anyone I have
ever cared about.
I am filled with the pollutants of the words I give myself.
And I am starving for love and attention,
but they get mad when I reach out.

6. ABC's

Around and around we went,
Behind the school of the playground,
Carefully hiding and yelling when found.
Dancing and shouting and smiling,
Everyone was everybody's friend.
Fun was the way to live
Giggles from every corner
Hellos and waves of goodbyes,
I guess it's time to say goodbye.
Juggling friends and fun and school
Killing innocence and my mood.
Loving and hating how I've changed.
Mourning the loss of childhood, at its grave.
Nobody said I'd have this pain.
Opening up to get closed again,
Proudly waiting for the days,
Quickly running for the safe,
Remembering how it was.
Swimming through the memories,
Tears trickle down my cheek.
Used to feel happy and unique.
Very worn out from growing up,
Where did the time go? I thought there was enough.
X-rays show how much my bones have grown,

Y do I feel stuck and alone?

Z the last letter of the alphabet, I learned that in the prime of my innocence.

7. The Countdown of Change

It's happening again
The rosy cheeks,
The flutter in my stomach
My eyes filled with gleam
In my mind there was no limit

But, it's happening again
What if he likes me,
They way that I like him
Maybe it's best to stay quiet.

It's happening again.
I can't eat, I can't think, I can't sleep.
I need to tell him.

It's happening again,
The butterflies release,

I'm glad I told him.

8. Flirty Deception is the Key to Misconception

My heart pounds when it hears your name
My lungs burst when they see you.
The atmosphere becomes elevated,
The oxygen becomes vague.
Little fairies dance in my head
And hearts are drawn around your name.
I am stuck on this coaster hanging from the loop,
No one is here to catch me,
But you, staring smiling too.
Nothing is what it seems
But oh for you darling,
I am willing to be deceived.

9. Exposure

*Carbon Monoxide tricks your body.
It binds to your red blood cells, and causes the block of
oxygen*

It's tasteless, colorless, has no smell,
Was that us?
It's been so long,
I can no longer tell.

All I know is that you were my defeat.
You had me fall,
Before I could even breathe.

You entered my life before I could get a say,
You filled the air,
And watched me suffocate.

I didn't know that I was exposed,
My life crashed like dominoes.
I started to feel a bit of pain, that's when I went down.
That's when you came.

The first headache should have been a sign

but I couldn't tell, I couldn't see, I thought I was fine.
My detector was off,
And soon I was exposed.

Clearly it's my fault for not being ready,
The worst exposers are the ones that are senseless.
It's not addiction, that's not the connection we had.
What happened was intoxication, a disclosure,
a defeat.

The carbon monoxide left me breathless,
Tricked my blood cells,
Let me believe-
it was good, but ultimately killed me in the end.
Caused a Teenage girl to be reckless.
My doom started to impend.

It's not just teenagers who get confused over what's
good for them,
our blood cells get confused too.

Mine were intoxicated, they were exposed to *you.*

10. We Were Not Self Evident

I met you and I knew,
This would be my downfall.
You lied, lied, lied but to me it was the truth.

Lately I've been feeling blue,
Should have never answered that phone call.
I met you and I knew.

I should have seen the clues
But I was blinded, you were my alcohol
You lied, lied, lied but to me it was the truth.

I trusted you and got screwed,
No one caught me in the trust fall.
I met you and I knew.

I fell too fast, no guidelines or reviews,
Aftermath of destruction, people say close call.
You lied, lied, lied but to me it was the truth.

I wish I never met you,
You made my eyes have waterfalls.

I met you and I knew.
You lied, lied, lied but to me it was the truth.

11. My Shards of Glass

Could you tell
That i fell
Before I told you?

Did you know
Before I'd know
That it wouldn't last?

Why would you love me
If you were going to leave?
My heart is heavy yet fragile,

I thought you would be gentle,
And I handed it to you.
You let it slip,
And within the cracks laid all of your fingerprints.

12. The Fear in Some

The goal is to keep moving.
Pawn by pawn, Girl by girl,
Then you ran into the queen,
The only one who challenged You,
The only one who made you weak.
You eliminated her so it would dispose of your feelings,
You knew that if you let her in, you would be losing.
She was the matrix of your philophobia
A girl with determination and stars in her eyes, a queen
among pawns and rooks,
She was less valued than a king- Yet when she spoke
everyone looked.
She was menacing to your macho
You were scared, you Coward, oh my bad...your honor,
Wow, if bowing down to a girl hurts your ego,
Shouldn't running away from one hurt your god
complex?
Point taken, to you she was just a girl, oh wait-I meant
object.

13. A Poem of Questions

Do you regret it?
Do you wish to forget?
Do you wish we never met?
Did you cry? Did you break?
Would you ever bleed to keep me safe?
Did you mean all the words you'd say?

Do you ever think it was a mistake?
Do you ever fear the sound of my name?
I asked myself these questions,
And it was hard to answer.

You showed me something,
You made me feel something,
And then turned as if I was nothing.

So I ask again;

Do you ever think it was a mistake?

You know who you are,
and to further prove it,
Your names _ _ a _ e.

14. Forgiveness

When your heart is ripped in pieces
But instead of shattering those who ripped you
You sew your heart back together
And the seam holding the pieces together is their name.
Like a beech tree my heart will grow but forever will
your name be engraved in me.
Forever will the stains of your fingerprints be tainted on
my pericardium
seeping all the way into my endocardium.
You entered the chambers of my heart
there's four. Two are for taking in blood, the other two
are for when it leaves,
you cut them all off , now there's only blood spilling out
of me.
You are now the second name to become a cicatrix on
me,
and you will never disappear,
instead you are the matrix of my misery.

15. Goodbye...

Walking.
Sand below her feet.
Sinking.
Waves latching onto
her hands.
Engulfed by the peace.
the peace. . .
the pieces of her . . .
drift away.

16. The Sun

The world orbiting the sun,
We are drawn in in by the light,
We survive because of the light,
And we die if we have too much.

She looked at you as if you were the sun.
She followed you because no matter what path
She was on,

She wanted you.
She needed you.
She breathed you,
She'd die for you.

You were the zapper,
She was the fly.
You were the sun,
She was the earth.
The closer she got the better chance of getting burned
The better chance of getting hurt.
But she was ready.

She needed you
She loved you

She breathed you
And she did die for you.

21

17. Her Ghost

Forever
 an
enigma
of
 the relation between your situation.
She sits in the crevice of your mind
owning a corner that's only hers.
She holds your lungs captive,
 and when you go to breathe it hurts.
Deep within the veins that connect your heart,
will be the knowledge of what you've done.
The clock ticks and ticks and ticks.
The breath of her words echo,
 the sound of her heels clicking the ground,
 the corners of her smile transition to a frown.
Why did you do it?
Who did you really hurt?
Letting her physically go was just an act of self harm,
because she sits staring, waiting, watching the life you
have undone.
Fear is the poison and you fed into the addiction
She was your girl, not your property
but together there was a life to vision.
She was a star and you were scared to get zapped

you shot her down,
So you did not feel trapped.
Instead you let go of her so you did not let go of your
own safety.
But now that she's gone she quite frequently haunts
your dreams
No words are said, just the repetition of a smile, a laugh
turn to a frown and a scream,
a girl meant for your life but now only stuck in your
dreams.
Forever an enigma
endlessly causing your misery.
Forever a spirit watching your indecency.

18. A Message I'll Never Send

Goodbye,
I forgive you,
I understand,
I hope your okay,
I love you.
I don't trust you.
I hate you.

Hello?
Are you there?
Will I see you again?
Did I mean anything?
You meant a lot to me.

I'm sorry it didn't work out.
I love you.

Even if it's your fault.

With love and hate from a 5 foot 1 girl
Kisses and hugs
From a rage filled girl.

Forgiveness, and goodbyes
But No
Trust and hellos,

Goodbye to the ass who brought hell
And hello to the girl who is stronger because of you.

Sincerely,
 A heart sewing back her arteries

19. My Tea is Steaming

The cardiovascular putty in my chest has been stretched
too thin.
The faucet I call my eyes has seized up.
The music box below my nose needs a new song.
I am no longer a toy to break,
I am no longer an appliance for when you need me,
I am no longer a song to sing when your free,
No more playing with my feelings
No more, no more, is all you're getting.

20. He is Not Here

The sun never shined so bright,
You never seemed so happy
The rain never looked so pretty
Your hand looked perfect in his

The sun never stung so bad
You couldn't look him in the eyes
The rain drowned you in seconds
His hand became a trigger

The sparkle in your eyes dimmed
You were nothing before and your nothing now
The rain on the window reflected the ones on your face
Baby girl, no one told you, but this was a game

The sun will rise again
You'll feel happy again
The rain will be refreshing
Your hand looks better without him

One day he'll regret it.

21. The girl I Was

The girl I was is gone,
She no longer roams these halls,
She doesn't breathe this air,
She doesn't smile or laugh or even cry the same.
The way she did her hair, the way she dressed, the way
she spoke,
She is no longer here.
The way her heart would beat, the way she would sing
on repeat-
Is gone.

Instead- what is left is me.
All the parts of her that survived.
I laugh, I smile, I cry.
But not the way I did when I was her.
Not the way I did before I was hurt.
I still sing, just not the same song.
The girl I was ...is gone,
she was lost in the waves of unkept promises and hands
that she would no longer hold.
She disappeared in the fog of gossip and desperation.
The girl I was drowned in one word replies and side
glances, she was dragged by holding hands, and what
she thought held her heart.

The girl I was couldn't fathom that somebody would play
with her heart,
The girl I was didn't think she could lose her own heart.

The girl I am now
Is still trying to be thankful for this.
Thankful for a lesson that the girl I was couldn't see.
After all everybody should get their heart broken,
That's how you find the real you,
That's how I found and am continuing to find the real
me.